Police Dogs

BY KARA L. LAUGHLIN

The Child's World

Published by The Child's World®
1980 Lookout Drive • Mankato, MN 56003-1705
800-599-READ • www.childsworld.com

ACKNOWLEDGMENTS
The Child's World®: Mary Berendes, Publishing Director
The Design Lab: Design
Jody Jensen Shaffer: Editing
Pamela J. Mitsakos: Photo Research

PHOTO CREDITS
© Andrew Burgess: leash; AP Photo/Stephen Chernin:
20; bikeriderlondon/Shutterstock.com: 8; Billy Gadbury/
Shutterstock.com: 16; duckeesue/Shutterstock.com: 18; Fotokon/
Shutterstock.com: 7; fstop123/iStock.com: 14; Jonpym/
Dreamstime.com: 11; KellyNelson/Shutterstock.com; 13; Marcel
Jancovic/Shutterstock.com: 9; John Roman/123RF.com: cover,
1; remik44992: bone; Tom Robinson/Dreamstime.com: 4;
X2Photo/iStock.com: 19

ISBN 9781626873100
LCCN 2014934480

Printed in the United States of America
Mankato, MN
July, 2014
PA02219

ABOUT THE AUTHOR

Kara L. Laughlin is the author of eleven books for kids. She lives in Virginia with her husband and three children. They don't have a dog...yet!

TABLE OF CONTENTS

This police dog stays inside the car until his handler tells him to come out.

Officers on Paws

Have you ever seen a police car with K-9 on it? Was there a dog in the back? What you saw was a police dog, or K-9 unit.

K-9 units help the police to fight and solve crime. Dogs can smell things better than people. They run faster than people. K-9 dogs are also loyal and brave. K-9 handlers teach dogs to use these strengths to fight crime.

INTERESTING FACT
Police dogs are called K-9s because K-9 sounds like canine. Canine is another word for dog.

A Rocky Start

People have used dogs to fight crime for a long time. In the Middle Ages, dogs were sent out at night to guard parts of Paris, France. The first trained police dogs were used in England in 1888. The police were trying to catch a man who was breaking a lot of laws. They tried to use two dogs to find the man. It didn't go well. One dog bit the police chief. Then both dogs ran away. But people didn't give up on police dogs. Soon many countries were training police dogs.

The first U.S. K-9 units were started in 1907 in New York City. They were mostly used to keep crowds from getting out of hand. By the 1970s K-9 units had special jobs. Some learned to find lost people. Some learned to sniff out drugs.

INTERESTING FACT

In the 1960s, police dogs attacked **civil rights** demonstrators. Pictures of the attacks were in newspapers all over. For a while after that, K-9s were not popular with the public.

This police dog is waiting for a command from his handler.

Police Dogs Today

Today, police dogs protect the public. They might go into schools to check for drugs. They might help find a lost child. Some dogs search for clues to help solve

This police dog is sniffing a bag for drugs.

crimes. Some can smell chemicals that are used to set buildings on fire. That helps the police to know if a fire was an accident or a crime.

Police dogs are trained to attack suspects.

Another thing police dogs do is to go after suspects. This can be bad for both the suspects and the dogs. When police dogs attack, they jump and bite. They don't let go until they get a command. But the suspect might have a gun or a knife. Dogs can get hurt or even killed while they are working.

INTERESTING FACT

If dogs are trained in another country, they learn that country's words. Their handlers keep using the same commands. It's easier for people to learn new words than it is for dogs!

What Makes a Good Police Dog?

Police dogs need to be healthy and strong. They need to like working. They need to have a strong **hunt drive** and **prey drive**. That means that they like to search for toys. When they find them, they like to bite and tug. K-9 dogs also need to be calm in new places. They need to be calm even in crowds. Some breeds with the right traits for police work are German shepherds, Doberman pinschers, beagles, border collies, and Belgian shepherds.

INTERESTING FACT

Some police dogs are bred to be guide dogs but aren't right for the job. They might have too much energy. They could be a little too protective. What makes a dog a bad guide dog could be the same thing that makes him a great police dog.

German shepherds like this one make great police dogs.

Training

Every police dog has a partner. They train together. All police dogs learn some of the same skills. They learn basic skills like sit, stay, and heel. They work at being quick and light on their feet. They practice being on the go for a long time.

Police dogs also get special jobs. Some learn to sniff for illegal drugs. Some learn how to find people. Some learn to search for clues to a crime. Some learn the smells of things that cause fires or make bombs. Many dogs are **dual purpose** K-9s. That means they learn two skills—like catching suspects and finding drugs.

Dogs in K-9 units don't know how important their jobs are. They think they are playing games. So when a dog is trained to find drugs, the trainer will hide a toy with some drugs. The dog learns that the toy will be where the smell of the drugs is. When the dog finds the toy, the trainer plays with the dog. The dog learns

This police dog in Canada is being trained to sniff for drugs.

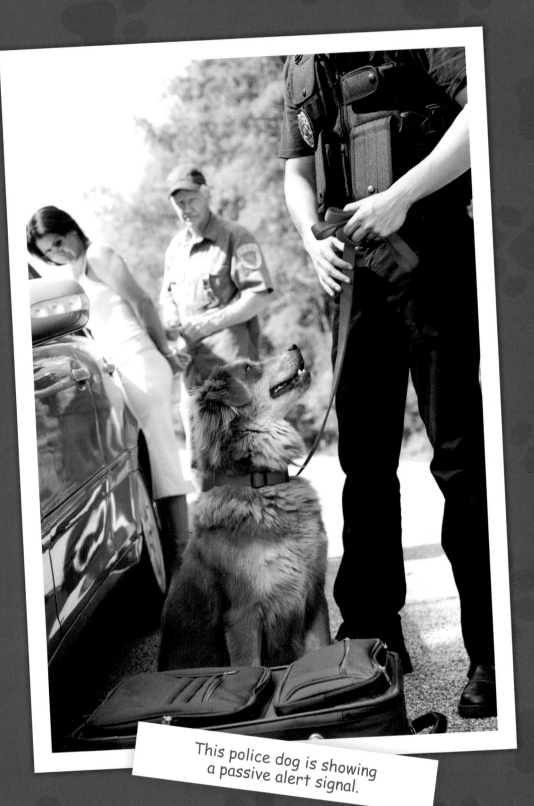

This police dog is showing a passive alert signal.

that every time he finds that smell, he will get to play. Training a dog to find bombs or people is done in a similar way.

Dogs learn to alert when they find what they are looking for. There are two kinds of alerts: **active alert** and **passive alert**. When a dog finds drugs, he begins digging and scratching to try to get to the drugs. That is the active alert. Sometimes it wouldn't be good for a dog to dig and scratch. What if the dog is looking for a bomb? He could set it off! Those dogs are trained to sit down where they find the right smell. This is a passive alert.

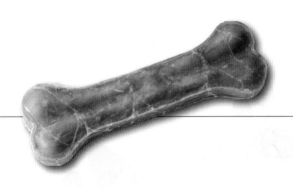

Life on the Force

Dogs in K-9 units live with their partners. When they are at home, they are off duty. At home, they are like any pet. At work, they are considered police officers.

Police dogs have badges just like their human partners.

They have badges. Some wear bulletproof vests. People who hurt or kill polices dogs can be sent to jail.

When they go to work, K-9s ride in a police car or truck made for a K-9 unit. The car has a metal cage built into it. The dog rides there to keep safe. Some days, the dogs just ride around all day. K-9s might not use their skills for days or weeks. Every week or two, a K-9 and his partner spend a full day training. That way they are always ready to help when needed.

INTERESTING FACT

If a dog dies in the line of duty, he gets a full funeral just like any other police officer. Some towns will fly their flags at half-mast to show respect for a K-9 that has fallen in the line of duty.

Meeting Police Dogs

If you see a police dog at school or at an event, be sure to ask first before petting the dog. Feel free to ask the officer questions. Most police officers like to answer questions about their K-9s. They think of it as part of their job.

Always ask first before approaching a police dog.

Bloodhounds like this one are often used to sniff for drugs or bombs.

K-9 Hero: Trakr

Can a dog be a superhero? If so, K-9 unit Trakr was one. Trakr lived in Canada with his partner, Jaymes Symington. Trakr worked as a K-9 for six years. He helped to arrest hundreds of people. He also found lost people. Trakr retired from the police force in May of 2001.

Here you can see James and Trakr searching the World Trade Center rubble.

On September 11, 2001, two planes hit the World Trade Center in New York City. Mr. Symington and Trakr went to New York City. They wanted to help look for survivors trapped when the towers collapsed. Tracker found someone the day they got to New York. She was the last survivor to be found at the World Trade Center. But Trakr didn't know that at the time. Trakr kept looking for two days. Then he collapsed. He was burned and sick from too much smoke. He went to a vet to get better.

Trakr returned to New York City. But Trakr's story didn't end. Mr. Symington heard of a contest for the "World's Most Clone-Worthy Dog." His essay on Trakr won the prize. The company that held the contest cloned Trakr. Trakr died in 2009. Later that year, Mr. Symington got five puppies with the same DNA as Trakr. Mr. Symington planned to train all five to be search-and-rescue dogs.

GLOSSARY

active alert (AK-tiv uh-LERT) When a dog digs and scratches to show that he's found what he's looking for.

civil rights (SIV-ull RYTS) Civil rights are the rights all people have to equal treatment.

dual-purpose (DOO-ull PUR-pus) Dogs trained in two or more special skills.

hunt drive (HUNT DRYV) A dog's urge to find prey that it can't see. A dog looking for a hidden treat uses hunt drive.

passive alert (PASS-iv uh-LERT) When a dog sits and stays to show he's found what he's looking for.

prey drive (PRAY DRYV) A dog's urge to catch prey that it sees. A dog catching a Frisbee uses prey drive.

LEARN MORE

IN THE LIBRARY

Baum, Elizabeth. *K-9 Police Dogs*. Mankato, MN: Amicus Publishing. 2013.

Bozzo, Linda. *Police Dog Heroes*. Berkeley Heights, NJ: Enslow Publishers. 2011.

Laughlin, Kara L. *Bomb-Sniffing Dogs*. Mankato, MN: The Child's World. 2014.

ON THE WEB

Visit our Web site for links about police dogs: *www.childsworld.com/links*

Note to Parents, Teachers, and Librarians: We routinely check our Web links to make sure they're safe, active sites—so encourage your readers to check them out!

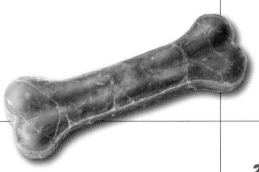

INDEX